D0491513

easystarters

easystarters

RYLAND
PETERS
& SMALL
LONDON NEW YORK

Designer Luana Gobbo

Commissioning Editor Elsa Petersen-Schepelern

Editor Sharon Ashman

Production Paul Harding

Art Director Gabriella Le Grazie

Publishing Director Alison Starling

First published in Great Britain in 2004
by Ryland Peters & Small
Kirkman House, 12–14 Whitfield Street
London W1T 2RP
www.rylandpeters.com

10 9 8 7 6 5 4 3 2 1

Text copyright © Maxine Clark, Clare Ferguson, Elsa Petersen-
Schepelern, Louise Pickford and Laura Washburn 2004
Design and photographs copyright © Ryland Peters & Small 2004

The authors' moral rights have been asserted. All rights reserved.
No part of this publication may be reproduced, stored in a retrieval
system or transmitted in any form or by any means, electronic,
mechanical, photocopying or otherwise, without the prior
permission of the publisher.

ISBN 1 84172 718 0

A CIP catalogue record for this book is available from the
British Library.

Printed in China.

Notes

All spoon measurements are level unless otherwise specified.

Ovens should be preheated to the specified temperature. If using
a fan-assisted oven, cooking times should be reduced according
to the manufacturer's instructions.

To sterilize preserving jars, wash them in hot, soapy water and
rinse in boiling water. Place in a large saucepan and then cover
with hot water. With the saucepan lid on, bring the water to the
boil and continue boiling for 15 minutes. Turn off the heat, then
leave the jars in the hot water until just before they are to be
filled. Sterilize the lids for 5 minutes, by boiling, or according to
the manufacturer's instructions. Jars should be filled and sealed
while they are still hot.

contents

getting started

When entertaining, whether you have planned an informal supper or a magnificent dinner party, you obviously want your meal to get off to a good start. The first course you serve is important because it sets the scene and hints at the delights to follow. Leaf through and you will soon see that *Easy Starters*, with its wide selection of delicious soups, salads, dips, meat, fish and vegetable dishes, has something to suit all tastes and every occasion.

Using only the freshest, spiciest and most colourful ingredients, the recipes here have a distinctly international flavour, with a range of starters from the Mediterranean, the Far East and the Middle East to choose from, together with some old favourites. What unites them all is that they are surprisingly quick and easy to prepare.

To take the stress out of your evening, many of the dishes can also be made well ahead of time and simply reheated as necessary once your guests have arrived. What's more, you will find that some of them can be adapted to make wonderful light lunches or great picnic, barbecue and party food. So, read on – *Easy Starters* is about to open a whole new world of stress-free entertaining.

SOUPS & SALADS

tomato soup

This soup needs to be made with really ripe, flavourful tomatoes – the best you can find. The citrus tang of the lemon will cut through the smoothness of the soup. Add some pesto and extra basil leaves to serve, for an Italian twist.

To skin the tomatoes, cut a cross in the base of each and dunk into a saucepan of boiling water. Remove after 10 seconds and put in a strainer set over a large saucepan. Slip off and discard the skins and cut the tomatoes in half around their 'equators'. Using a teaspoon, scoop out the seeds into the strainer, then press the pulp and juice through the strainer and transfer to a blender. Discard the seeds. Chop the tomato halves and add to the blender.

Purée the tomatoes, adding a little of the stock to help the process – you may have to work in batches. Add the remaining stock, season to taste with salt and pepper and transfer to the saucepan. Heat well without boiling. Serve in heated soup plates and top each serving with 1 teaspoon lemon juice, 1 tablespoon pesto, if using, chives or basil, lemon zest and pepper.

1 kg very ripe red tomatoes

500 ml chicken stock, or to taste

sea salt and coarsely crushed black pepper

TO SERVE

shredded zest and freshly squeezed juice of 1 unwaxed lemon

4 tablespoons pesto (optional)

scissor-snipped chives or torn basil

SERVES 4

cream of mushroom soup

A few dried porcini will give a stronger flavour to a soup made with regular cultivated mushrooms. Use large portobellos to give a deeper colour as well as flavour.

Put the dried porcini in a bowl, add 250 ml boiling water and let soak for at least 15 minutes. Heat the oil in a frying pan, add the fresh mushrooms and sauté until coloured but still firm. Reserve a few slices for serving.

Add the onion to the frying pan and sauté until softened, then add the garlic, nutmeg and parsley. Rinse any grit out of the porcini and strain their soaking liquid several times through muslin or a tea strainer. Add the liquid and the porcini to the pan. Bring to the boil, then transfer to a food processor. Add 2 ladles of the boiling stock, then pulse until creamy but still chunky.

Heat the butter in a saucepan until melted, stir in the flour and cook gently, stirring constantly, until the mixture is very dark brown (take care or it will burn). Add the remaining stock, 1 ladle at a time, stirring well after each addition. Add the mushroom mixture, bring to the boil, then simmer for 20 minutes. Season with salt and pepper to taste. Serve in heated soup bowls topped with a few reserved mushrooms, parsley and crème fraîche.

Note If you use a blender to make soup, the purée will be very smooth. If you use a food processor, it will be less smooth, and if you use the pulse button, you can make the mixture quite chunky, which suits mushrooms.

25 g dried porcini mushrooms

4 tablespoons olive oil

6 large portobello mushrooms, wiped, trimmed and sliced

1 onion, halved and thinly sliced

3 garlic cloves, crushed

a pinch of freshly grated nutmeg

leaves from a large bunch of fresh parsley, finely chopped in a food processor

1.25 litres boiling chicken or vegetable stock

4 tablespoons butter

4 tablespoons plain flour

sea salt and freshly ground black pepper

TO SERVE

4–6 tablespoons coarsely chopped fresh parsley

4–6 tablespoons crème fraîche

SERVES 4–6

An old-fashioned nourishing soup, full of healthy green things. If you do not have sorrel growing in your garden (or available in your supermarket), it can be omitted.

kitchen garden soup

1 fresh bay leaf

1 small cabbage, quartered

60 g unsalted butter

2 leeks, halved and sliced

1 onion, chopped

2 teaspoons salt

250 g new potatoes, chopped

a handful of fresh flat leaf parsley, chopped

250 g fresh shelled peas

1 Little Gem lettuce, quartered and thinly sliced

a bunch of sorrel, sliced

sea salt and freshly ground black pepper

unsalted butter and/or crème fraîche, to serve (optional)

SERVES 4–6

Put the bay leaf in a large saucepan of water and bring to the boil. Add the cabbage quarters and blanch for 3 minutes. Drain the cabbage, pat dry and slice thinly.

Heat the butter in a large saucepan. Add the cabbage, leeks, onion and 2 teaspoons salt and cook until softened, 5–10 minutes. Add the potatoes, parsley and 2 litres water. Add salt and pepper to taste and simmer gently for 40 minutes.

Stir in the peas, lettuce and sorrel and cook for 10 minutes more. Taste for seasoning. Ladle into heated soup bowls, add 1 tablespoon butter and/or crème fraîche, if using, to each bowl and serve.

gazpacho

4 Lebanese cucumbers, halved lengthways, deseeded, peeled and chopped*

6 tomatoes, skinned and chopped

1 large red onion, chopped

1 red pepper, deseeded and chopped

1 garlic clove, finely chopped

125 g bread, crusts removed (optional)

3 tablespoons red wine vinegar

3 teaspoons salt

1 litre iced water

3 tablespoons olive oil

1 tablespoon tomato purée or harissa paste

TO SERVE

3 thick slices good bread, crusts removed, cut into cubes

1 onion, finely chopped

1–2 Lebanese cucumbers, halved, deseeded and chopped (skin left on)

1 green or red pepper, deseeded and finely chopped

2 hard-boiled eggs, chopped

2 ripe tomatoes, halved, deseeded and chopped

olive oil, for frying

SERVES 6

The classic, chilled summer soup of Spain has dozens of variations, depending on its area of origin. The traditional way of serving it is in a large tureen with six separate dishes of garnishes served alongside – these are added by the guests at the table, according to taste. Chop each garnish coarsely rather than finely – the soup should have some texture to it.

Put the peeled cucumbers, tomatoes, onion, pepper, garlic, bread, if using, vinegar and salt in a food processor (which gives more texture than a blender). Add the iced water and blend, in batches if necessary, until coarsely chopped, then ladle into a bowl. Mix the olive oil and tomato purée or harissa paste in a small bowl, then whisk it into the soup. Chill until ready to serve, but for at least 3 hours.

Meanwhile, heat some olive oil in a frying pan, add the bread cubes and sauté, turning frequently, until crisp and golden on all sides. Watch them, because they burn easily. Remove from the pan, drain on kitchen paper and set aside.

When ready to serve, put each garnish in a separate small bowl, along with a spoon. Serve the soup in the tureen or in soup plates and let your guests add their own selection of garnishes to their soup.

Note *The cucumbers are peeled and a red pepper, rather than a green one, is used in this version of the soup – red tomatoes and a green pepper and green cucumber skins blended together make a rather unappetizing greyish-brown. However, to be authentic, use these green elements.

tuscan panzanella

There are as many variations of this Tuscan bread salad as there are cooks – some old recipes don't even include tomatoes. The trick is to let the flavours blend well without allowing the bread to disintegrate into a mush. Always use the ripest, reddest, most flavourful tomatoes you can find – sweet Marmande, with its furrowed skin, is a great choice, or you could use one of the full-flavoured heirloom varieties, such as Black Russian or Green Zebra, or at least an Italian plum tomato.

Cut the tomatoes in half, spike with slivers of garlic and transfer to a roasting tin. Roast in a preheated oven at 180°C (350°F) Gas 4 for about 1 hour, or until wilted and some of the moisture has evaporated.

Meanwhile, put the bread on an oiled stove-top grill pan and cook until lightly toasted and barred with grill marks on both sides. Tear or cut the toast into pieces and put in a salad bowl. Sprinkle with a little water until damp.

Add the tomatoes, cucumber, onion, parsley, salt and pepper. Sprinkle with the olive oil and vinegar, toss well, then set aside for about 1 hour to develop the flavours.

Add the basil leaves and caperberries or capers and serve.

6 very ripe plum tomatoes

2 garlic cloves, sliced into slivers

4 thick slices day-old bread, preferably Italian-style, such as pugliese or ciabatta

about 10 cm cucumber, halved lengthways, deseeded and thinly sliced diagonally

1 red onion, chopped

1 tablespoon chopped fresh flat leaf parsley

8–12 tablespoons extra virgin olive oil

2 tablespoons white wine vinegar, cider vinegar or sherry vinegar

a bunch of fresh basil, leaves torn

12 caperberries or 4 tablespoons capers packed in brine, rinsed and drained

sea salt and freshly ground black pepper

SERVES 4

chicory salad
with roquefort, celery and walnuts

4–5 heads of chicory, about 600 g, halved, cored and thinly sliced

2 celery stalks, thinly sliced, plus a few leaves, torn

75 g Roquefort cheese, crumbled

50 g shelled walnuts, chopped

a handful of fresh flat leaf parsley, finely chopped

1 baguette, sliced, to serve

WALNUT VINAIGRETTE

2 tablespoons wine vinegar

1 teaspoon fine sea salt

1 teaspoon Dijon mustard

7 tablespoons sunflower oil (see method)

1 tablespoon walnut oil (optional)

freshly ground black pepper

SERVES 4

This salad is a combination of robust flavours and it's a sophisticated way to get your meal started. Developed unintentionally by a gardener at the Brussels botanical gardens in the middle of the nineteenth century, chicory is now cultivated for a good part of the year, and modern varieties have none of the bitterness of their ancestors. When buying, choose very pale chicory with only a hint of green; they grow in the dark, so colour on the leaves is a sign that they have been exposed to the light and are not as fresh. Also, big is not necessarily better – 20 cm is the maximum length for best taste.

To prepare the vinaigrette, put the vinegar in a salad bowl. Using a fork or a small whisk, stir in the salt until almost dissolved. You may have to tilt the bowl so the vinegar is deep enough to have something to stir. Mix in the mustard until completely blended. Add the oil, 1 tablespoon at a time, beating well between each addition, until emulsified. If you're using the walnut oil, use 1 less tablespoon of sunflower oil. Stir in pepper to taste.

Just before you're ready to serve the salad, add the chicory, celery, Roquefort, walnuts and parsley to the vinaigrette and toss well. Serve immediately, with a basket of sliced baguette.

tomato salad
with anchovy vinaigrette

750 g ripe vine tomatoes

1 large shallot or 1 small red onion, thinly sliced

coarse sea salt and freshly ground black pepper

ANCHOVY VINAIGRETTE

1 garlic clove

½ teaspoon Dijon mustard

2 tablespoons white wine vinegar

6 canned anchovy fillets, rinsed and drained

8 tablespoons extra virgin olive oil

a small handful of fresh basil leaves

TO SERVE

a handful of fresh flat leaf parsley, finely chopped

a few fresh basil leaves, torn

SERVES 4

Anchoïade is a Provençal anchovy sauce/dip, which is spread thickly on grilled bread slices, or served with raw vegetables as a starter. Here it becomes a dressing for what will hopefully be very ripe, flavourful tomatoes. If these are not available, use boiled baby new potatoes instead and toss while the potatoes are still warm. Serve this tomato version with a chilled Provençal rosé and lots of crusty bread.

To make the anchovy vinaigrette, put the garlic, mustard, vinegar and anchovies in a small food processor and blend well. Add the oil, 1 tablespoon at a time, then blend in the basil. Season with pepper and set aside.

Cut the tomatoes into quarters or eighths, depending on their size. Arrange on a plate and sprinkle with the shallot or red onion. Season lightly with salt, then spoon the vinaigrette over the top. Sprinkle with the parsley, basil and freshly ground black pepper and serve at room temperature.

caesar salad

1 egg, preferably free range and organic

6 smallest leaves of cos lettuce (a young cos, not Little Gem)

½ tablespoon freshly squeezed lemon juice, plus 1 lemon cut into wedges, to serve (optional)

2 tablespoons extra virgin olive oil

3–4 canned anchovy fillets, rinsed and drained

Parmesan cheese, at room temperature, shaved into curls with a vegetable peeler

sea salt and freshly ground black pepper

CROUTONS

1 thick slice crusty white bread or challah bread

2 tablespoons oil and/or butter, for cooking

1 garlic clove, crushed

SERVES 1

This is probably the most famous salad in the world, with the perfect combination of salty, crispy crunch. Note that this recipe serves one person – just multiply the ingredients according to the number of guests you have.

To cook the egg, put it in a small saucepan, cover with water and bring to the boil. Reduce the heat and simmer for 4–5 minutes. Remove from the heat and cover with cold water to stop it cooking further. Let cool a little, then peel. Cut into quarters just before serving.

To make the croutons, tear the bread into bite-sized chunks, brush with oil or butter and rub with the garlic. Cook on a preheated stove-top grill pan until crisply golden and barred with brown.

Put the lettuce in a large bowl and sprinkle with salt and pepper, add the lemon juice and toss with your hands. Sprinkle with olive oil and toss again.

Put the croutons in a bowl and put the dressed leaves on top. Add the anchovies, egg and Parmesan, sprinkle with pepper and serve with lemon wedges, if using.

Note Originally, the salad used a one-minute egg – coddled, rather than boiled – so that the egg became part of the dressing. These days, some people are nervous about uncooked eggs, so this recipe calls for a boiled egg, simmered for 4–5 minutes after the water has come to the boil. The white will be set, but the yolk still soft and creamy.

avocado salad

Avocado is a fabulous salad ingredient – so creamy and delicious, it can really be used as a dressing in itself. You can mix avocado with whatever looks good that day – prawns, crab, smoked fish or smoked chicken pulled into shreds. Just top it with a few herb leaves if they're handy, grind lots of pepper over it, maybe add a squeeze of lemon juice, and eat it without any dressing.

If using pancetta, cut the slices into 3–4 pieces. Heat a frying pan, brush with the 1 tablespoon olive oil, add the pancetta or pancetti and cook over medium heat, without disturbing, until crisp on one side. Using tongs, turn the slices over and fry until crisp and papery but not too brown. Remove and drain on kitchen paper.

Put the dressing ingredients in a salad bowl and beat with a fork or small whisk. When ready to serve, add the leaves to the dressing and turn using your hands. Cut the avocados in half and remove the stones. Using a teaspoon, scoop out balls of avocado into the salad. Toss gently if you like (though this will send the avocado to the bottom of the bowl). Add the crispy pancetta or pancetti and serve.

Notes To test an avocado for ripeness, don't stick your thumb in it. Instead, cradle it in the palm of your hand and squeeze gently. If it just gives to the pressure, it's perfect.

It's not true that keeping the stone in guacamole or any other avocado dishes will stop them going brown. However, lime juice, lemon juice or vinegar will. Add avocado to dishes at the very last minute so it has no chance to discolour.

6 very thin slices smoked pancetta or bacon, or about 200 g pancetti cubes (lardons)

250 g salad leaves – a mixture of soft, crisp and peppery

1–2 ripe Hass avocados

1 tablespoon olive oil, for frying

DRESSING

6 tablespoons extra virgin olive oil

1 tablespoon cider vinegar or rice vinegar

1 garlic clove, crushed

1 teaspoon Dijon mustard

sea salt and freshly ground black pepper

SERVES 4

DIPS & BREADS

A wonderful combination of fresh spring flavours and colours. Puréeing the peas gives a sweet, earthy base on which to sprinkle the combination of salty, nutty Pecorino (Parmesan would work very well here, too) and fruity pears tossed in a few drops of balsamic vinegar for sharpness. A delicious start to a light dinner party.

pear, pecorino and pea crostini

1 Italian sfilatino or thin French baguette, sliced into thin rounds

250 g shelled fresh or frozen peas

freshly grated nutmeg

1 small ripe pear

a drop of balsamic or sherry vinegar

125 g fresh young Pecorino or Parmesan cheese, diced

extra virgin olive oil, for brushing and moistening

sea salt and freshly ground black pepper

SERVES 6

To make the crostini, brush both sides of each slice of bread with olive oil and spread out on a baking sheet. Bake in a preheated oven at 190°C (375°F) Gas 5 for about 10 minutes until crisp and golden.

Meanwhile, blanch the peas in boiling water for 3 minutes if they are fresh or 2 minutes if they are frozen. Drain them, refresh in cold water and drain again. Put the peas in a food processor or blender and process to a purée, moistening with a little olive oil. Season to taste with salt, pepper and freshly grated nutmeg.

Core and finely chop the pear. Mix with a drop of balsamic or sherry vinegar, then add the cheese and mix well.

Spread the crostini with a mound of pea purée and top with a spoonful of the pear and cheese mixture. Serve immediately.

char-grilled aubergine dip

1 large aubergine

2 tablespoons extra virgin olive oil

1 teaspoon ground cumin

200 ml plain yoghurt

2 spring onions, finely chopped

1 tablespoon freshly squeezed lemon juice

sea salt and freshly ground black pepper

toasted pita bread, to serve

SERVES 6

Cut the aubergine lengthways into thin slices, about 2 mm thick. Put the oil in a small bowl, add the cumin, salt and pepper, mix well, then brush all over the aubergine.

Cook on a preheated stove-top grill pan or under a hot grill for 3–4 minutes on each side until charred and tender. Let cool, then chop finely.

Put the yoghurt in a bowl, then stir in the aubergine, spring onions and lemon juice. Taste and adjust the seasoning with salt and pepper. Serve in bowls or on plates, with toasted pita bread for dipping.

This spicy aubergine dip is like baba ganoush, the Middle Eastern aubergine purée, only with yoghurt instead of tahini. The aubergine should be charred well to achieve the best smoky flavour.

egg, mascarpone and asparagus crostini

This is a creamy light topping, packed with the flavour of asparagus. For the best results, don't be tempted to make this with anything other than fresh asparagus. If you have some truffle oil, you can drizzle a little over for a special occasion, as the flavours of eggs and truffle go superbly well together.

1 Italian sfilatino or thin French baguette, sliced into thin rounds

125 g unsalted butter, softened

4 tablespoons chopped fresh parsley

4 spring onions, finely chopped

12 spears fresh asparagus, stems trimmed

6 large eggs

4–6 tablespoons mascarpone cheese, softened

extra virgin olive oil, for brushing

truffle oil, for drizzling (optional)

sea salt and freshly ground black pepper

SERVES 6

To make the crostini, brush both sides of each slice of bread with olive oil and spread out on a baking sheet. Bake in a preheated oven at 190°C (375°F) Gas 5 for about 10 minutes until crisp and golden.

Meanwhile, beat the butter with the parsley and spring onions and season with salt and pepper.

Cook the asparagus in boiling salted water for about 6 minutes until tender. Cut off and reserve the tips and slice the stems.

Boil the eggs for 6–8 minutes. Plunge into cold water for a couple of minutes, then peel and roughly mash with a fork. Add the spring onion mixture and mascarpone and stir until creamy. Fold in the sliced asparagus stems, then season with salt and pepper.

Spread the egg mixture thickly onto the crostini, top with the asparagus tips and drizzle with a couple of drops of truffle oil, if using, or some extra virgin olive oil. Serve immediately.

toasted focaccia
with borlotti beans and greens

Good, toasted bread, with a coarse mash of beans on top and a handful of wild salad leaves, is a country treat. If you don't have time to soak and cook the dried borlotti beans, use canned beans. Dandelion leaves can sometimes be found in good greengrocers, but if you can't find them, use other greens such as frisée, rocket or watercress instead.

4 slices focaccia, sliced about 1.5 cm thick

2 garlic cloves, crushed

4 tablespoons extra virgin olive oil

400 g canned borlotti beans*

1 teaspoon sea salt flakes

1 teaspoon freshly ground black pepper

2 handfuls of fresh wild dandelion leaves or other bitter salad leaves, about 25 g

freshly squeezed juice of 1 lemon

SERVES 4

Toast the bread on both sides, preferably on a preheated stove-top grill pan or barbecue. While still hot, rub the toast on one side with a crushed garlic clove and drizzle with half the oil. Keep hot.

Put the remaining oil in a saucepan and heat gently. Add the remaining garlic and fry briefly until aromatic but not brown. Add the drained, cooked beans and mash coarsely with a fork. Add the salt and pepper and cook, stirring, until heated through.

Put the hot toast onto 4 serving plates, spoon the bean mixture on top, then add a tangle of leaves. Sprinkle with lemon juice and serve while the toast is warm, the beans hot and the salad still bouncy.

To serve as party food, cut small squares of bread to make tiny versions of this dish.

Note *If you are using dried beans, use about 200 g. Soak them overnight in cold water to cover, then drain. Put in a large saucepan, cover with boiling water and return to the boil. Reduce the heat and simmer until done, 1½–2 hours, depending on the age of the beans.

VEGETARIAN

deep-fried baby artichokes

This delicious dish is very simple and very stylish. It calls for tiny globe artichoke heads, preferably with violet petals and no more than 5 cm long. Try it: it is a fascinating recipe, perfect for spring. You could serve the artichoke quarters on individual plates for an elegant dinner party starter or, for a more informal gathering of family and friends, let your guests help themselves from a large communal platter which is passed around the table.

10–12 tiny globe artichokes, preferably with stalks attached

virgin olive oil, for frying

TO SERVE

lemon wedges

sea salt and freshly ground black pepper

SERVES 4–6

Cut the artichokes into quarters lengthways.

Fill a saucepan with the olive oil to a depth of 5 cm. Heat to about 190°C (375°F) or until a small cube of bread turns brown within 40 seconds.

Add the artichokes 6–8 quarters at a time and, using a slotted spoon, push them down hard against the bottom of the pan. Fry until they are crisp and smell caramelized. Carefully remove with tongs or a slotted spoon and drain, stems upward. Keep hot or warm while you cook the remainder.

Remove the stalks and serve the frizzled heads sprinkled with salt and pepper and with lemon wedges for squeezing.

crudités

Crudités are a classic French starter, especially in Parisian cafés and bistros. The selection of vegetables here is fairly representative, but it does vary. Canned corn and tuna are common, as are hard-boiled eggs. You could also try blanched asparagus tips, sliced cherry tomatoes or wafer-thin red onion slices.

To make the vinaigrette, put the vinegar in a bowl. Using a fork or a small whisk, stir in the salt until almost dissolved. You may have to tilt the bowl so the vinegar is deep enough to have something to stir. Mix in the mustard until completely blended. Add the oil, 1 tablespoon at a time, whisking well between each addition, until emulsified. Add pepper to taste. Set aside.

Heat the vinegar in a wok. As soon as it boils, remove from the heat, add the red cabbage and toss well. Salt lightly and set aside until the cabbage turns an even deep-fuchsia colour.

Meanwhile, put the potatoes in a saucepan with cold water to cover. Bring to the boil, add salt and cook until tender, about 15 minutes. Drain, let cool slightly, then peel and slice thinly.

Bring another saucepan of water to the boil, add salt, then the beans. Cook until just tender, 3–5 minutes. Drain and set aside.

Put the carrots, lemon juice and a pinch of salt in a bowl and toss well; set aside. Cut the beetroot in quarters lengthways, then slice thinly to get small triangular pieces. Peel the cucumber (if you like), cut it in quarters lengthways and slice.

Arrange small mounds of each ingredient on plates, alternating colours. Add a few spoonfuls of vinaigrette to each one and sprinkle with parsley. Serve with a basket of sliced baguette.

2 tablespoons wine vinegar

¼ red cabbage, thinly sliced

250 g baby new potatoes

125 g baby green beans, topped and tailed

3 medium carrots, grated

1 tablespoon freshly squeezed lemon juice

3 cooked beetroot

175 g cucumber

a handful of fresh flat leaf parsley, finely chopped

fine sea salt

1 baguette, sliced, to serve

VINAIGRETTE

3 tablespoons wine vinegar

1 teaspoon fine sea salt

2 teaspoons Dijon mustard

11 tablespoons sunflower oil

freshly ground black pepper

SERVES 4

baby leeks
with herb vinaigrette

Light lovely leeks in a lively herb-studded sauce. Serve these at the start of a substantial spread, to allow room for expansion, or as part of a light lunch with a savoury tart, for example. If you can't find sorrel, it will be a shame, but the recipe works without, so don't feel obliged to replace it with anything.

750 g baby leeks

2 shallots, thinly sliced

a small bunch of chives, scissor-snipped

VINAIGRETTE

60 ml wine vinegar

1 teaspoon Dijon mustard

1 teaspoon fine sea salt

250 ml sunflower oil

a small handful of fresh flat leaf parsley

a small handful of watercress

a small handful of tarragon

3 sorrel leaves

freshly ground black pepper

SERVES 4

Put the leeks in the top of a steamer and cook for 7–10 minutes until tender. Remove and set aside to drain.

To make the vinaigrette, put the vinegar, mustard and salt in a small food processor and blend well. Add about 75 ml of the oil and blend for a few seconds. Continue adding the oil, bit by bit, and blending until the vinaigrette is emulsified. Add the parsley, watercress, tarragon and sorrel and pulse again to chop. Add pepper to taste.

If the leeks are still too wet, pat dry with kitchen paper. Arrange in a serving dish, spoon the vinaigrette over the top and sprinkle with shallot slices and chives. Serve with any remaining vinaigrette on the side.

pan-grilled aubergines
with pine nuts and garlic

Aubergines are a versatile vegetable, popular all over the world. Look for really fresh ones, which should be glossy and firm to the touch. New breeds have little of the traditional bitterness, so need no pre-salting. This is a quick, light and easy starter.

Cut the aubergines lengthways into thin slices just under 1 cm thick, about 12–16 in total. Using a fork, score both sides of each slice several times in a criss-cross pattern. Brush a little olive oil on both sides of the slices.

Preheat a ridged stove-top grill pan or non-stick frying pan until very hot. Drizzle with a few teaspoons of the remaining oil. Cook half the aubergine slices, pressing them down firmly, for about 3 minutes on each side or until tender and firmly griddle-marked. Remove from the pan, roll them up loosely and keep them warm. Repeat with the remaining slices.

Add the pine nuts to the oiled, hot pan and toast gently, stirring them about to prevent scorching. Remove from the pan and set aside.

Finally, put the remaining olive oil in a bowl, add the chopped mint, garlic, if using, and sea salt and mix to form a dressing.

Serve the aubergines drizzled with dressing, sprinkled with the pine nuts and dotted with the remaining mint sprigs.

Variation Add sun-dried or semi-dried (sun-blushed) tomatoes and a little of their rosy oil.

2 medium aubergines, about 700 g total

90 ml extra virgin olive oil

75 g pine nuts

a small bunch of fresh mint, half chopped, half in sprigs

4 garlic cloves, crushed (optional)

½–1 tablespoon sea salt

SERVES 4

warm goats' cheese soufflés

Served warm, these soufflés are a favourite starter for the cook because you don't have to panic about getting them to the table before they sink! Make sure you butter the ramekins very well so that you can get the soufflés out.

Melt the butter in a saucepan, add the flour and cook over low heat for 30 seconds. Remove the pan from the heat and gradually stir in the milk until smooth. Return to the heat and stir constantly until the mixture thickens. Cook for 1 minute.

Remove from the heat and let cool slightly. Beat in the cheese, egg yolks, herbs and salt and pepper to taste. Put the egg whites in a bowl and whisk until soft peaks form. Fold the egg whites into the cheese mixture.

Spoon the mixture into the ramekins and bake in a preheated oven at 200°C (400°F) Gas 6 for 15–18 minutes until risen and golden on top. Remove from the oven and let cool for about 15 minutes.

Using a palette knife, work around the edges of the soufflés and turn them out onto plates. Serve with rocket salad.

25 g unsalted butter

2 tablespoons plain flour

250 ml milk

100 g soft goats' cheese

3 eggs, separated

2 tablespoons chopped fresh mixed herbs, such as basil, chives, mint and tarragon

sea salt and freshly ground black pepper

rocket salad, to serve

6 ramekins, 200 ml each, well buttered

SERVES 6

FISH & SEAFOOD

salmon rillettes

Rillettes are a traditional French dish that usually features shredded pork or duck, but salmon and other oily fish offer a delicious substitute. This makes a perfect, hassle-free starter or alternatively use it as a topping for party canapés.

Put the salmon fillet, skin side up, in a wide saucepan just big enough to fit the fish. Cover with the fish stock. Add the bay leaves, heat to simmering, then poach the fish for 7 minutes. Remove the pan from the heat and let the fish cool in the liquid. Drain the fish and peel off the skin.

Melt 40 g of the butter in a frying pan, add the smoked salmon and sauté until just opaque. Cool completely.

Using a fork, shred both salmons together. Put the remaining butter in a bowl and beat with an electric beater or wooden spoon until very soft (butter at room temperature makes this easier). Add the salmons and peppercorns and beat together. Taste and season well with salt. Press the mixture into the 6 small pots, level the tops with the back of a knife if you like, then refrigerate until set and firm.

Remove from the refrigerator 15 minutes before serving so the pâté can return to room temperature. Serve with Melba toast.

500 g salmon fillet, skin on

600 ml fish stock

3 fresh or dried bay leaves

350 g unsalted butter, at room temperature

350 g smoked salmon, unsliced and cut into chunks

1 tablespoon green peppercorns, crushed

sea salt

Melba toast, to serve

6 small pâté pots

SERVES 6

Thai fish, prawn or crab cakes are quick and easy to make – perfect as a first course. If you have time, marinate the prawn mixture for 30 minutes or so. Keep a few jars of chilli jam on hand, but you can use a prepared chilli sauce if you prefer.

thai prawn cakes
with chilli jam

To make the chilli jam, put the tomatoes, chillies and garlic in a food processor and blend until fairly smooth. Transfer the mixture to a saucepan, add the ginger, soy sauce, sugar, vinegar and salt and bring to the boil. Reduce the heat slightly and simmer fast for 30–35 minutes, stirring occasionally until thick and glossy.

Warm the sterilized jars in a low oven, pour in the thickened jam and let cool completely. Seal and store in the refrigerator. Use within 1 month.

To make the prawn cakes, put the prawns in a food processor and blend to a purée. Add the lime leaves, spring onions, coriander, egg, fish sauce and rice flour, blend briefly, then transfer the mixture to a bowl. Using damp hands, shape into 24 patties, 5 cm diameter.

Fill a frying pan with oil to a depth of 1 cm, heat for 1 minute over medium heat, then add the cakes, spacing them well apart. Fry in batches for 2 minutes on each side until golden brown. Remove the cakes with a slotted spoon and drain on kitchen paper. Keep them warm in a low oven while you cook the remainder. Serve with chilli jam or sweet chilli sauce.

500 g uncooked, shelled prawns

4 lime leaves, very finely chopped

4 spring onions, finely chopped

2 tablespoons chopped fresh coriander

1 egg

1 tablespoon Thai fish sauce

50 g rice flour

peanut or sunflower oil, for frying

Chilli Jam (below) or sweet chilli sauce, to serve

CHILLI JAM

500 g ripe tomatoes, coarsely chopped

3–4 red chillies, coarsely chopped

2 garlic cloves, chopped

1 teaspoon freshly grated ginger

2 tablespoons light soy sauce

250 g palm sugar or soft brown sugar

100 ml white wine vinegar

½ teaspoon sea salt

2 preserving jars, about 200 ml each, sterilized (page 4)

SERVES 6 (MAKES 24 CAKES)

drunken clams

Try to find the small vongole clams, which tend to be sweeter and more tender than the larger varieties. This recipe will serve four as a starter, but you can serve it with other Asian dishes plus rice and noodles for an impressive banquet.

Tap each clam lightly on the work surface and discard any that won't close. Put the clams in a saucepan and add the stock, rice wine or sherry, garlic, ginger, spring onions and chilli. Grind Szechuan pepper over the top and bring to the boil. Cover with a lid and let steam for 3–4 minutes until all the shells have opened.

Discard any unopened clams and transfer the rest to warmed bowls. Strain the stock through a fine sieve, pour over the clams, then serve.

2 kg fresh clams, well scrubbed

150 ml fish or vegetable stock

100 ml Shaohsing (sweetened Chinese rice wine) or sweet sherry

4 garlic cloves, sliced

3 cm fresh ginger, peeled and sliced

6 spring onions, sliced

1 red chilli, deseeded and sliced

Szechuan pepper or freshly ground black pepper

SERVES 4

fresh vietnamese spring rolls

Vietnamese food is full of flavour and not as oily as Chinese. These fresh spring rolls are delicious. They can be made several hours in advance, then sprayed with a mist of water before being covered with clingfilm to stop them drying out. A great hands-on starter.

To make the dipping sauce, put the garlic, chilli and sugar in a spice grinder and blend to a purée. Alternatively, put them in a mortar and pestle and grind to a paste. Add the chopped lime and any collected juice and purée again. Stir in the fish sauce and about 125 ml water. Set aside.

To make the spring rolls, first assemble all the ingredients on platters and fill a wide bowl with hot water. Work on one roll at a time.

Dip 1 ricepaper wrapper in the water for about 30 seconds until softened. Put on a plate (not a board, which will dry out the ricepaper). Put a small pinch of each ingredient in a line down the middle of the wrapper, fold over both sides of the wrapper, then roll up like a cigar. (If you find it easier to fold only one side, as shown, let some of the ingredients protrude from the other end.)

Spray with a mist of water and set aside on a plate, covered with a damp tea towel, while you prepare the others.

To serve, spray with water again and serve with the dipping sauce.

Notes *The wrappers come in packs of 50 large or 100 small. Wrap leftover wrappers in 2 layers of plastic and seal well.

**If you like, stir 1 tablespoon sesame oil through the noodles after soaking.

24 small Vietnamese ricepaper wrappers (16 cm)*

30 g cellophane noodles (1 small bundle), soaked in boiling water for 20 minutes, drained, then snipped into 5 cm lengths**

3 carrots, thinly sliced into matchstick strips

1 mini cucumber, halved, deseeded and thinly sliced into matchstick strips

6 spring onions, halved and thinly sliced lengthways

2 punnets enoki mushrooms

fresh mint leaves

fresh coriander leaves

1 small packet fresh beansprouts, trimmed, rinsed and dried

300 g cooked crab meat, or 300 g peeled, chopped prawns or 300 g stir-fried pork mince

NUÓC CHAM DIPPING SAUCE

2 garlic cloves, crushed

1 red chilli, deseeded and chopped

1 tablespoon caster sugar

½ lime, quartered, deseeded and chopped

1½ tablespoons fish sauce

SERVES 12 (MAKES 24 ROLLS)

Peppers are ubiquitous ingredients in Italian antipasti dishes. They respond well to grilling and roasting, two methods that develop the natural sugars. Mixed with salty anchovies and sharp pickled caperberries or capers, they really come into their own. This recipe is from southern Italy – easy, elegant and delicious.

peperoni farciti

4 red or yellow peppers, quartered lengthways and deseeded

16 canned anchovy fillets, rinsed and drained

16 caperberries or 2 tablespoons capers, rinsed and drained

a small bunch of fresh marjoram or oregano, chopped

2 tablespoons extra virgin olive oil

freshly ground black pepper

SERVES 4

Arrange the quartered peppers in a large roasting dish or tin.

Using scissors or a small knife, cut each anchovy fillet in half lengthways. Put 2 strips into each pepper segment. Add a caperberry or a share of the capers to each segment and sprinkle with the chopped herbs and olive oil.

Roast, uncovered, towards the top of a preheated oven at 180°C (350°F) Gas 4 for 20–30 minutes or until wrinkled, aromatic and beginning to char a little at the edges. Serve hot, warm or cool, sprinkled with pepper.

Note Use any colour pepper other than green – green tastes too acidic.

MEAT & POULTRY

Yoghurt-crusted chicken on skewers is a delicious way to start a meal. The yoghurt tenderizes the chicken and helps the lemon soak into the meat. In summer, cook them on a barbecue – the yoghurt becomes delicious and slightly crunchy. Otherwise, cook them under a hot grill.

chicken lemon skewers

Cut the chicken fillets lengthways into 2 mm thick strips and put in a shallow ceramic dish.

Put all the marinade ingredients in a bowl, stir well and pour them over the chicken. Turn the chicken to coat it, then cover and let marinate in the refrigerator overnight.

The next day, thread the chicken onto the soaked bamboo skewers, zigzagging the meat back and forth as you go.

Cook on a preheated barbecue or under a hot grill for 3–4 minutes on each side until charred and tender. Let cool slightly before serving.

500 g skinless chicken breast fillets

MARINADE

250 ml plain yoghurt

2 tablespoons extra virgin olive oil

2 garlic cloves, crushed

grated zest and freshly squeezed juice of 1 unwaxed lemon

1–2 teaspoons chilli powder

1 tablespoon chopped fresh coriander

sea salt and freshly ground black pepper

12 bamboo skewers, soaked in cold water for 30 minutes

SERVES 4

chicken liver pâté

This simple, semi-smooth pâté is excellent served as a starter, or as a snack or on a picnic. It's incredibly quick to make – it takes less than 10 minutes. It can be eaten warm, but is usually better cooled and chilled (use the freezer for speed). Decorate the butter seal with some peppercorns and extra sprigs of thyme.

Heat one-third of the butter in a non-stick frying pan. Add the livers and sauté over high heat for 2 minutes, stirring constantly. Standing well back from the pan, carefully add the brandy and light it with a match. Let flame for 1–2 minutes, shaking the pan, then add the garlic, onion, salt and nutmeg and cook for a further 2 minutes until the liquid has almost all evaporated and the livers and onion are golden. (Ideally, the livers should still be pink inside.) Add the thyme and another one-third of the butter and heat until the butter has melted.

Transfer the mixture to a food processor. Blend, in 4–5 short bursts, to a semi-smooth paste. Spoon into 1 large or 6–8 small china pots. Smooth the surface with a knife. Melt the remaining butter. Pour it over the pâté, adding a decorative topping of thyme and peppercorns, pushing them into the butter.

Let cool, then put in the freezer for at least 1 hour. Transfer to the refrigerator and chill for 1–2 hours until very cold and firm. Serve the same day with Melba toast or crisp, toasted slices of baguette, or store longer. Flavours improve for up to 1 week.

150 g salted butter, cubed

250 g chicken livers, trimmed and halved

4 tablespoons brandy

2 garlic cloves, crushed

1 onion, chopped

½ teaspoon sea salt flakes

¼ teaspoon freshly ground nutmeg

2–3 tablespoons fresh thyme leaves

TO SERVE

sprigs of fresh thyme

about 20 peppercorns

Melba toast or slices of baguette, toasted

1 large or 6–8 small china pots

SERVES 6–8

rumaki bacon and chicken liver skewers

This easy but sophisticated starter comes from Hawaii, which has a lively, constantly evolving, multi-cultural cuisine. Rumaki shows Japanese and Chinese influences, combined with a European touch and typical Polynesian style, exploiting the different cooking styles to excellent effect.

3 tablespoons dark soy sauce

2 tablespoons sake or dry sherry

1 tablespoon soft dark brown sugar

2 teaspoons ground ginger

250 g chicken livers, trimmed

8 slices rindless smoked streaky bacon, halved

150 g canned water chestnuts, drained and sliced*

8 spring onions, trimmed and quartered

16 bamboo skewers or medium satay sticks, soaked in cold water for at least 30 minutes

SERVES 4

Mix the soy sauce, sake or sherry, sugar and ginger in a large shallow glass or china dish. Using scissors, cut the livers into 16 equal pieces, discarding any discoloured areas.

Push one end of a piece of bacon onto a soaked skewer or satay stick. Add a piece of liver, 2 water chestnuts, both at once (take care that they don't split), and some spring onion pieces set crossways. Pull the bacon lengthways, stretching it tightly around the pieces on the skewer or satay stick and securing it back again at the first end so that it neatly encloses the entire rumaki contents in a little parcel. (Slide the whole little parcel to one end if it makes it easier.)

Set the completed rumaki in the marinade and turn to coat. Continue until all 16 are made. Marinate for at least 10 minutes, then turn and marinate for another 10 minutes. (Alternatively, marinate for 8 hours in the refrigerator.)

Preheat a grill or barbecue until very hot. If using a grill, cover the grill tray with oiled foil. Cook the rumaki 10 cm from the heat for 4–6 minutes on each side or until they are deep, dark brown. Pour over the extra marinade as they are turned. Serve hot.

Note *If only sliced canned water chestnuts are available, use 3–4 slices per skewer or stick.

vietnamese pork balls
with chilli dipping sauce

500 g pork mince

6 garlic cloves, crushed

2 stalks lemongrass, thinly sliced

1 bunch coriander, finely chopped

2 fresh red chillies, deseeded and chopped

1 tablespoon brown sugar

1 tablespoon fish sauce, such as *nam pla*

1 egg, beaten

peanut oil, for frying

sea salt and freshly ground black pepper

CHILLI DIPPING SAUCE

125 ml white rice vinegar

2–6 small or 1 large red chilli, thinly sliced

1 tablespoon fish sauce

1 spring onion, thinly sliced (optional)

½–1 tablespoon brown sugar

SERVES 6 (MAKES ABOUT 12 BALLS)

A delicious traditional recipe that's perfect for an informal start to a meal or a drinks party. The original recipe is manna from heaven to the dedicated chilli-head, but the amount used here is plenty for most tastes. Use fat Fresno chillies for a mild flavour, or tiny bird's-eye chillies for blinding heat. Fish sauce is used as a seasoning in Vietnamese cooking – like using salt or soy sauce. If you can't find it, use salt instead (not as interesting, but okay at a pinch).

To make the chilli dipping sauce, mix all the ingredients in a small bowl, stir to dissolve the sugar, then set aside to develop the flavours.

To make the pork balls, put all the remaining ingredients, except the peanut oil, in a bowl and mix well.

Dip your hands in water, take 1–2 tablespoons of the mixture and roll it into a ball. Repeat with the remaining mixture. Put the balls, spaced apart, on a plate as you finish them. Chill for at least 30 minutes.

Fill a wok one-third full of peanut oil and heat to 190°C (375°F) or until a cube of bread browns in 30 seconds. Add the pork balls 6 at a time and deep-fry in batches until golden brown. Remove and drain on crumpled kitchen paper, keeping them warm in the oven until all the balls are done.

Serve with the chilli dipping sauce.

bresaola and rocket
with olive oil and parmesan

Bresaola is Italian cured, air-dried beef – flavourful, deep crimson, lean and succulent. Preferably it should be cut from the piece, sliced very thinly, but it is also available pre-sliced, in packs. This combination of mellow, salty meat with the sharp, savoury taste of Parmesan and best-quality extra virgin olive oil is simple, but wonderful. It's a deliciously easy way to get a meal started.

12–16 thin slices of bresaola

50 g piece of Parmesan cheese

a large handful of wild rocket

4–6 teaspoons best-quality extra virgin olive oil

SERVES 4

Divide the slices of bresaola equally between 4 serving plates.

Using a vegetable peeler or sharp knife, shave off thin curls of the Parmesan and drop them on top of the bresaola.

Add the rocket, then drizzle with extra virgin olive oil and serve immediately.

index

credits

Recipes

Maxine Clark
Pear, pecorino and pea crostini
Egg, mascarpone and asparagus crostini
Salmon rillettes

Clare Ferguson
Rumaki: bacon and liver skewers
Chicken liver paté
Bresaola and rocket with olive oil and Parmesan
Toasted focaccia with borlotti beans and greens

Peperoni farciti
Deep-fried artichokes
Pan-grilled aubergines with pine nuts and garlic

Elsa Petersen-Schepelern
Caesar salad
Avocado salad
Tuscan panzanella
Cream of mushroom soup
Tomato soup
Gazpacho
Fresh Vietnamese spring rolls
Vietnamese pork balls

Louise Pickford
Thai prawn cakes with chilli jam
Char-grilled aubergine dip

Chicken lemon skewers
Warm goats' cheese soufflés
Drunken clams

Laura Washburn
Kitchen garden soup
Tomato salad with anchovy vinaigrette
Chicory salad with Roquefort, celery and walnuts
Crudités
Baby leeks with herb vinaigrette

Pictures

Key: a=above, b=below, r=right, l=left, c=centre

Martin Brigdale 13, 16, 19–20, 31, 37–38
Peter Cassidy Front endpapers, 1, 2–3, 5r, 6l & b, 7, 8–9, 10–12, 14–15, 17, 22–25, 28–29, 32–33, 34–35, 36, 39–42, 45r, 47–48, 52–58, 60, 62
Jean Cazals 9r
Vanessa Davies 18
Gus Filgate Back endpapers, 4–5, 26–27, 30
Jeremy Hopley 50
William Lingwood 44–45, 46, 51, 61
David Munns 6a, 27r, 43, 63
Debi Treloar 21, 35r
Ian Wallace 49
Simon Walton 59